WOMEN OF THE BIBLE

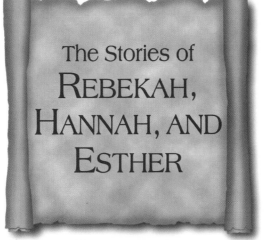

The Stories of
REBEKAH,
HANNAH, AND
ESTHER

RETOLD BY
CARINE MACKENZIE

A BIBLETIME GIFT COLLECTION

An Inspirational Press Book for Children

Rebekah

THE MOTHER OF TWINS

Rebekah was a beautiful girl who grew up with her brother Laban in the land of Padanaram, which we now call Syria. She was a good and dutiful daughter and helped her father Bethuel and her mother with the household tasks.

One of her daily duties was to fetch water for the house from the well. Each evening she would go to the well with a pitcher or big jug on her shoulder.

One evening Rebekah went to the well as usual. Just as she finished filling her jug, a man came near. "Please let me drink a little water from your jug," he said.

"Drink, my Lord," Rebekah replied politely and quickly gave him some water. When the man had drunk enough to satisfy his thirst, Rebekah said to him, "I will draw water for your camels, too." Rebekah worked hard, drawing from the well as much water as the thirsty camels could drink.

When the camels had finished drinking, the man gave Rebekah a valuable gift—a gold earring and two gold bracelets. "Please tell me whose daughter you are," he said. "Would there be room in your father's house for me and my men to stay for the night?" Rebekah replied, "I am Bethuel's daughter. Of course, we have enough straw for your camels, plenty of food for you and your men and enough room for you to stay."

The man bowed his head and prayed to God. He believed and was thankful that God was guiding him in his journey and helping him to do his job.

You too can ask God to help you with your work. Remember to thank him when he does help you.

Rebekah ran home ahead of the man to tell her family to prepare for some guests.

When the brother Laban saw Rebekah's beautiful gifts he knew that the visitor was someone special. He rushed out to welcome him. "Come in," he said, "everything is ready for you."

The visitor washed his feet which would be dusty after traveling. Then a meal was set down before him. But he said, "I will not eat anything until I have told you why I am here."

"My master Abraham has sent me from the land of Canaan back to his native land to find a suitable wife for his son Isaac. He assured me that the Lord God would guide me all the way. So I asked the Lord for a sign.

"If a girl came, who would give me water and also offer to give water to my camels, I would know that she was the right girl for Isaac.

"No sooner had I said this," the man continued, "when Rebekah came down to the well and gave me and the camels all the water we needed. When I asked about her family I was so thankful to learn that the Lord had guided me to the family of my master's brother. Will you agree to Rebekah becoming Isaac's wife?"

Laban and Bethuel both agreed that God had arranged everything. They could not find any fault. "We will allow Rebekah to become your master's son's wife," they said.

The man bowed down and worshipped God. He then brought out gold and silver jewels and lovely clothes for Rebekah and her family. Only when his work was done did he sit down and enjoy his evening meal.

The visitor stayed with Bethuel overnight and in the morning he was anxious to start the return trip to Canaan. Laban and his mother were sad to see Rebekah leaving them so soon. "Let her stay for a few days yet, at least ten," they said. But the servant was keen to get back to his master with the good news. "Let's ask Rebekah herself," they said. "Will you go with this man?" they asked. "I will go," she replied firmly.

God is also asking you a question. Will you follow the Lord Jesus and love him? What is your answer?

Rebekah started out on her new life
that very day. Her only companion
was her nurse Deborah. She left
her family and her home and made
the journey to a strange land to
marry a man she had never seen.
This was God's plan and purpose
for her life.

Your life is in God's hands. He has
a plan for you too.

One evening Isaac was out in the peace and quiet of the field thinking and praying to God. When he looked up he saw a train of camels coming near. When Rebekah noticed this young man she asked the servant who he was. "That is my master Isaac," she was told. She jumped down from the camel and after covering her face with a veil, as was the custom, she walked to meet Isaac. The servant informed Isaac about all that had happened. Isaac loved Rebekah very much and they were married right away. Rebekah was a great comfort to Isaac whose mother Sarah had recently died.

Isaac and Rebekah were married for nearly twenty years but they still had no baby boy or girl. Isaac prayed to God and asked him to give them a child. God heard this prayer and Rebekah was soon expecting—not one baby but twins. Before they were born, Rebekah asked God about her expected children. God told her that her sons would be two different nations and that the younger one would be more important than the elder one.

Rebekah's twin sons were very different in appearance. Esau was born first. He was red and quite hairy. His brother Jacob was smooth-skinned.

As Esau was older he would have certain privileges known as his birthright including a special bless-ing from his father.

As the boys grew up they were still very different in their appearance and their interests. Esau loved being out in the country, hunting wild animals and bringing home venison for his father to eat. But Jacob had a quieter nature and pre-ferred to stay closer to home. He was his mother's favorite.

One day Esau came home from hunting absolutely starving. Jacob had been cooking and Esau could smell the lovely aroma of hot lentil soup. "Give me some of your soup, please, I am nearly fainting," said Esau. "I shall give you food, if you will agree to give me your birthright," replied Jacob.

"I am dying of hunger," gasped Esau. "Of what use is my birthright to me?" So the agreement was made. Esau got some bread and lentil soup and Jacob received the birthright.

One day Rebekah overheard a con-
versation between Esau and his
father Isaac who was now growing
blind. "I am getting old," Isaac said,
"and I do not know when I may die.
Take your bow and arrow, Esau,
and go out and hunt. Bring back
some venison to make my favorite
meal. After I eat it, I will bless you
before I die."

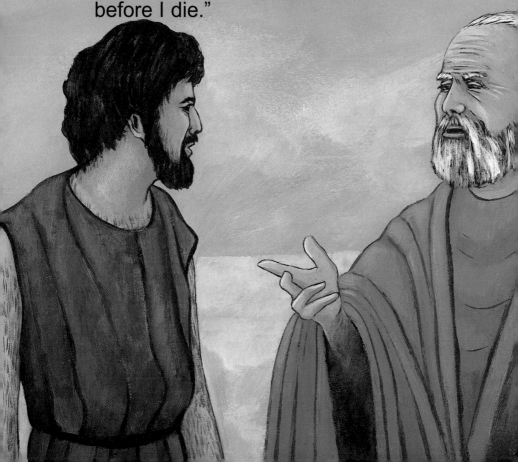

As soon as Esau had departed on his hunting trip, Rebekah hurried to find Jacob. "Now do what I tell you, Jacob," she said. "Go to the flock and bring me two good young goat kids: I will make a tasty dish, just the way your father likes it. After he has eaten he will bless you instead of Esau." Was she remembering what God had told her years before about the younger son being more important than the older?

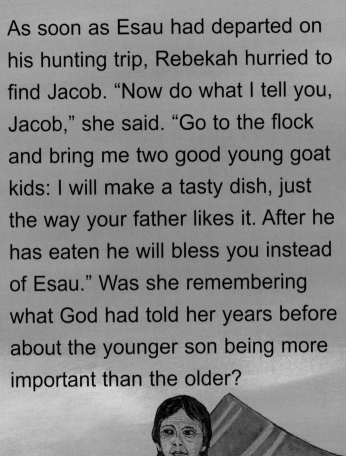

"But Esau has a hairy skin and I am smooth," objected Jacob. "If father finds out that I am deceiving him, he will probably curse me, and not bless me." But Rebekah urged Jacob. "Just do as I say. If there is any curse, it will be on me."

So Jacob did as Rebekah wanted.
Soon the lovely savory meat was
ready. Rebekah took some of
Esau's best clothes and helped
Jacob dress in them. Then she took
the skins of the kids which had
been used to make the stew and
covered Jacob's hands and neck.
They did not feel so smooth now.
They felt rough and hairy—more
like Esau's.

Jacob went to Isaac's tent with the meat and some bread. "My father," he said. "Who is that," replied the blind Isaac. "I am Esau your first-born son," lied Jacob. "I have done as you asked. Come and eat this venison, and bless me."

"How did you manage to find it so quickly, my son?" asked Isaac.

"The Lord God brought it to me," continued Jacob. Jacob sinned when he told lies. If you tell a lie that is also a sin. Often one lie leads to another.

Isaac was not sure, so he said, "Come a little nearer to me so that I can feel if it really is Esau." Jacob must have been scared. Rebekah must have been anxious too, wondering what was happening. Isaac was puzzled. "The voice sounds like Jacob but the hands feel like Esau," he said.

So Jacob and Rebekah's trick was not found out. After Isaac had eaten the meal Jacob came and kissed his father, and Isaac blessed Jacob, asking God to provide for and make him prosper.

Almost as soon as Jacob had left his father, brother Esau came back from his hunting trip. He prepared the venison stew and brought it to his father. "Who are you?" exclaimed Isaac. "I am Esau, of course," he replied. Isaac was quite taken aback. "Then who has just been here and given me venison stew and received my blessing— and indeed will be blessed?" Esau was heartbroken when he heard this. "Can you not bless me too, father?" he begged. "My brother has taken away my birthright and now my blessing too."

Isaac answered, "I have said that he will be lord over his brother and that will come to pass." Esau hated his brother for this and vowed to kill him.

When Rebekah heard this she called for Jacob and said, "Esau is planning to kill you. You had better escape to Haran. My brother Laban will give you a place to live. Once Esau's anger has cooled down, I will send for you."

Isaac agreed with Rebekah and urged Jacob to go to his mother's old home.

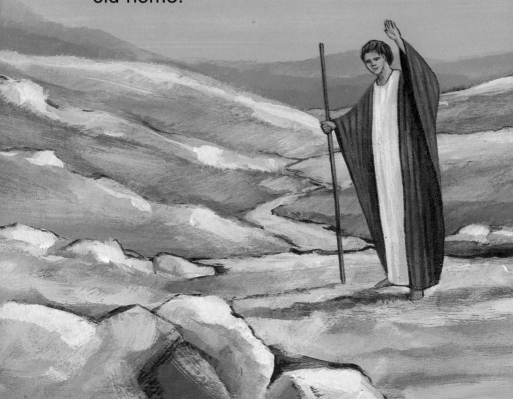

Jacob had many adventures in the years that followed. Many years later he met with Esau again and made peace. When Jacob returned with his large family, Isaac was still living. Rebekah never saw her favorite son Jacob again. She died and was buried in a cave in a field called Machpelah.

Rebekah and Jacob were very close but even the closest human friends must part one day. If you have the Lord Jesus Christ as your friend, he will never leave you nor forsake you. He is the best friend you could ever have.

Hannah

THE MOTHER WHO PRAYED

Hannah lived in the country of Israel many years ago. She was married to a good man called Elkanah and they lived in the town of Ramah. In those days some good men had more than one wife. Elkanah had another wife called Peninnah who had several sons and daughters.

Hannah's greatest sorrow was that she did not have a child. How she longed to have a baby son of her own.

Every year Elkanah took his family
to Shiloh to worship the Lord God in
His temple.

God wants us also to worship Him,
both in church and at home, by
singing praise to Him, reading the
Bible and praying to Him.

Each year, at Shiloh, Elkanah gave
gifts to all his family. Peninnah and
her boys and girls all received a gift
but Hannah received a special gift
because he loved her best of all.

No gift could make Hannah forget that she did not have a child of her own. Peninnah mocked her for not having any children. This made poor Hannah feel even more miserable. You may know just how Hannah felt. It can be very upsetting to have someone mocking you.

Hannah could not eat her food and often cried. Not even Elkanah, who loved her so much, could comfort her.

"Why are you crying?" he asked her. "Why do you not take something to eat? Why are you so sad? Am I not better to you than ten sons could be?"

But Elkanah could not really help her with her problem. Hannah knew that the only one who could help her was the Lord God.

One day, when they were in Shiloh, Hannah made her way alone to the temple of the Lord. She felt very sad. In the temple she wept and prayed and told all her problems to the Lord.

In her prayer, she made a promise to the Lord: "If you will remember me and give me a baby boy, I will give him back to work for the Lord for all his life."

While Hannah was praying Eli the priest was sitting on a seat by a pillar of the temple. He noticed Hannah and watched her closely. He thought she looked very strange. As she prayed in her heart, her lips moved but no sound came from her mouth, so Eli thought she had drunk too much wine. He went to Hannah and said to her, "How long are going to be drunk? Stop drinking so much wine!" Hannah turned to him and said, "I am a very sad woman. I have not been drinking wine at all. I am in great distress and have been telling the Lord all about it."

Eli realized his mistake and said to her, "Go away in peace and may God give you what you have asked for."

"I hope you will always think kindly of me," Hannah replied.

Hannah believed that God would answer her prayer and she went back to the house very happy indeed. She did not look sad anymore. She felt so much better that she began to eat her food again.

What a difference it had made to Hannah to tell her problem to the Lord God. Today too you can take your problems to God. You can tell Him all your worries because He asks you to do so. He promises to help you if you trust in Him.

The next day Elkanah and his family rose early in the morning. They went to the temple to worship the Lord. Then they set off back to their own home in Ramah.

After some time Hannah had a baby son of her own and she was very happy indeed. God had answered her prayer. Hannah did not forget that she had asked God for this baby, for she called him Samuel. Samuel means "asked of God."

The next time that Elkanah went to Shiloh to worship the Lord, Hannah did not go with him. "I will stay at home with Samuel," she said to her husband. "I will take him to Shiloh when he is a little older. Then I will give him to the Lord and he will stay there always." Elkanah agreed with Hannah. "Yes," he said, "you do what you think best. Wait until Samuel is old enough."

So when Samuel was a little older, Hannah took him to the house of the Lord in Shiloh. Hannah went to Eli the priest and reminded him of their last meeting. "I am the woman that you saw praying here to the Lord. I prayed for this child and the Lord gave me what I asked for. I am now keeping my promise and returning the child to work for the Lord."

So Samuel stayed in the temple
with Eli from that day on. He
learned to help Eli, who was an old
man, with many little tasks.

He also worshipped God in the temple. We must not think that it is only grown-up people who have to worship God. Boys and girls also must worship Him.

When Hannah was in trouble, you remember, she prayed to God to help her. Now that she was happy, she did not forget God. She prayed again telling Him how happy and joyful she felt. She knew that God was holy and great and strong. She also praised God and said, "There is no one so great as God. God has made the whole world and rules over everyone."

Hannah knew that God had given her a son. She wanted to praise Him for His goodness. You should remember to pray to God not only when you are in trouble but when you are happy too. You should praise God for all His goodness. God wants you to thank Him for all His good gifts to you. He has given you life, a home and food. But the greatest gift of all is His Son Jesus. God gave His only beloved Son Jesus so that all who believe in Him will be saved from their sins and live forever with Him in heaven.

Elkanah and Hannah went back to Ramah. They left Samuel at Shiloh with Eli. He worked for the Lord there, just as his mother had promised.

Each year after that Hannah still went with Elkanah to Shiloh to worship in the house of the Lord. How she would look forward to seeing Samuel again. Every time she went she brought him a little coat that she had made for him.

Hannah willingly gave her son to work for God but she was not left without any children at home. God rewarded her by giving her more children: three boys and two girls.

You will remember that Hannah's prayer for her son was that he would serve the Lord in the temple. This prayer was answered too. Day by day Samuel served God in the temple and was a true servant of God. God soon showed that He loved Samuel.

One evening Eli, who was now nearly blind, went to bed as usual. After he had finished his tasks, young Samuel also went to bed. As he lay there, all of a sudden he heard a voice calling his name.

He thought that it was Eli who was calling him. "Here I am," he answered, as he ran to Eli. "You were calling me."

"I did not call you," Eli replied. "Go back to bed again."

Again he heard someone calling "Samuel!" Samuel rose again and went to Eli. "Here I am," he said, "for you did call me."

"I did not call you," said Eli. "Lie down again."

God was calling to Samuel but Samuel did not know this.

Samuel heard the voice again calling his name for the third time. "Here I am for you did call me," he said to Eli.

This time Eli knew that the voice that Samuel was hearing was the voice of God. "Go and lie down," Eli said to Samuel, "and if He calls you again say, 'Speak Lord, for your servant is listening.'"

God did speak to Samuel again. He told him that Eli's sons were very wicked. Eli did not punish them or stop them, so the whole family was to be punished.

Samuel lay in bed, thinking about what had happened. In the morning he rose as usual to open the big doors of the temple, but was afraid to tell Eli what God had said to him.

But, Eli called for Samuel and asked him what God had said to him. "Do not hide anything from me," he said. Samuel told him everything. Eli's humble reply was, "It is the Lord: let Him do what seems best to Him."

Hannah's son served the Lord as a young boy all his life. When he grew up he continued serving and became an important man of God: all in answer to his mother's prayers. Hannah loved God so much that she did not keep her son for herself. Hannah was also a woman with a problem. She prayed to God about that problem and God helped her. God is still the same today. He tells you to take your problems to Him.

Esther

THE BRAVE QUEEN

Esther was a very beautiful Jewish girl. Her people had been taken away by force from their own land, so Esther lived in the land of

Persia which today we call Iran.
Esther's mother and father were
both dead and she had been
brought up by her uncle's son, a
kind man called Mordecai.

Ruling over Persia was the mighty king Ahasuerus. He had a wonderful palace in Shushan, with white, green and blue curtains, fastened with silver rings to marble pillars and rich marble floors colored red, blue, white and black.

Ahasuerus made a grand feast for all his princes and servants. There was plenty of food and drink. After seven days of eating and drinking, the king gave the order that Vashti the queen was to come from her rooms in the palace, into the dining hall so that all the princes could admire her beauty.

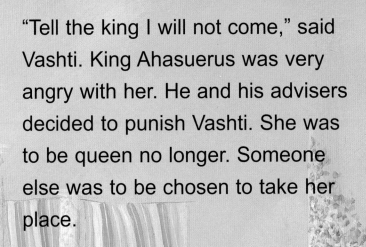

"Tell the king I will not come," said Vashti. King Ahasuerus was very angry with her. He and his advisers decided to punish Vashti. She was to be queen no longer. Someone else was to be chosen to take her place.

A notice was sent out through the land. Any beautiful young girl who would like to become queen should come to the palace in Shushan. The king would choose the one he liked best.

Many girls flocked to the royal
palace and among them was
Esther. She spent a whole year in
the palace preparing to meet the
king. Every day Mordecai walked
past the courtyard of Esther's house
to find out if all was well.

Eventually it was Esther's turn to go to the king. When he saw her, he loved her more than anyone else. He put the royal crown on her head and made her the queen, instead of Vashti. He made a great feast in her honor. But no one in the palace knew that she was a Jewish girl. Mordecai had thought it wiser that she kept that secret. Esther did as Mordecai asked.

One day Mordecai overheard two of the king's officers plotting to kill king Ahasuerus. Mordecai told Esther and she reported it to the king giving Mordecai the credit. The report was investigated and found to be quite true. Both men were hanged. The whole story was written in the royal record books.

The most important person in the king's service was a proud man called Haman. Every time he passed by, the people would bow down to him—everyone except Mordecai. Mordecai was a Jew, who bowed down only to God. We too must worship only God and not allow anyone or anything else to take His place. Haman was enraged by this insult. He was so angry he wanted to get rid of all the Jews from the land, especially Mordecai.

Wicked Haman made up a law that every Jewish person throughout the land, young and old, men, women, and children, would be killed on a certain day, eleven months later. The king agreed to the law and copies of it were sent throughout the land.

Mordecai heard the terrible news. He put on coarse, rough garments instead of his own clothes and put ashes on his head to show how sad he was. He cried loudly and bitterly.

News was brought to Esther that her cousin was sitting outside the gate in a sorry state. Esther was very upset. She sent out some nice new clothes to Mordecai but he refused to take them.

Esther sent Hatach, her special servant, to find out what was Mordecai's problem. Mordecai told him all about Haman's wicked plot. He gave a copy of the law for Esther to see for herself.

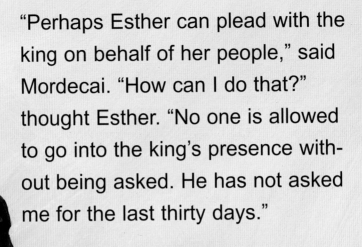

"Perhaps Esther can plead with the king on behalf of her people," said Mordecai. "How can I do that?" thought Esther. "No one is allowed to go into the king's presence without being asked. He has not asked me for the last thirty days."

Mordecai urged Esther to think of something. "You would be killed too," he said.

"Who knows, but you may have been made queen so that you could do something now."

God had Esther's life in His plan. He knew each step. God has your life in His plan too. Everything is known to Him.

Esther sent back her reply to Mordecai. "Gather all the Jews in the town of Shushan and fast for three days. I and my maids will do the same. Then I will go to see the king. And if I die, I die."

But Esther did not die. When she went to see the king three days later he was pleased to see her. He held out his golden scepter, which was a sign that she could come near him.

How amazing to think that we can speak to the King of Kings at any time. We can pray to God and tell Him our problems and He will listen to us and help us.

"What do you want, queen Esther?" asked Ahasuerus. "You can have anything you wish, even half of my kingdom."

"I would like you and Haman to come to a banquet today," replied Esther.

"Certainly," said the king. "Tell Haman to hurry to a banquet prepared by Esther," he ordered.

Esther did not tell the king yet of her problem. At the feast, he again asked her what she would like from him. Perhaps she felt the time was not right or perhaps she was afraid.

She said, "I would like the king and Haman to come to another banquet tomorrow."

Haman was highly delighted with this special honor. The only thing that spoiled his enjoyment was the sight of Mordecai at the king's gate, standing straight and tall as he went past. Mordecai would not bow down to him. When Haman went home he boasted to his wife and family of how favored he was by the king and queen Esther. "But all these honors are worth nothing to me, so long as I see that Jew Mordecai."

"You should get rid of Mordecai," they all suggested. "Build a big gallows seventy-five feet high and have Mordecai hanged."

"What a good idea," thought Haman. "I will do that straight away." What a wicked man Haman was. But things did not work out as Haman had expected. God's timing is perfect. He has all His creatures and all their actions in His care.

That night the king could not sleep.
"Bring a book and read it to me," he
ordered. One of the record books
was brought and the story of how
Mordecai had uncovered the plot to
kill Ahasuerus was read out. The
king was very interested to hear
this. "What honor has been done to
Mordecai to show my gratitude?"
"Nothing has been done," he was
told.

"Something must be done right away. Is there any official about at this time of night?"

Ahasuerus was told that Haman was there. "Good, bring him to me, at once," the king said.

"Haman, I want to honor someone. What would be the best way to do that?" asked the king.

"Oh," thought Haman. "Surely he means to honor me."

"Well," said Haman. "A good idea would be to let the man wear your royal robes and royal crown and be led on your horse through the city streets."

"Hurry up and do just that to Mordecai, the Jew, who sits at my gate."

Haman was shocked. How horrified he felt giving this honor to the man he hated so much.

While he was telling his wife and friends of his misfortune, he was hastily called to Esther's second banquet.

Esther entertained the king and the wicked Haman at another lovely meal. The king asked her again, "What can I do for you?"

"Oh King," replied Esther. "Please spare my life and the lives of my people. A plot has been hatched to kill all the Jewish people. If we were only to be sold as slaves, I would have held my tongue."

"Who has decided to do this?" demanded Ahasuerus.

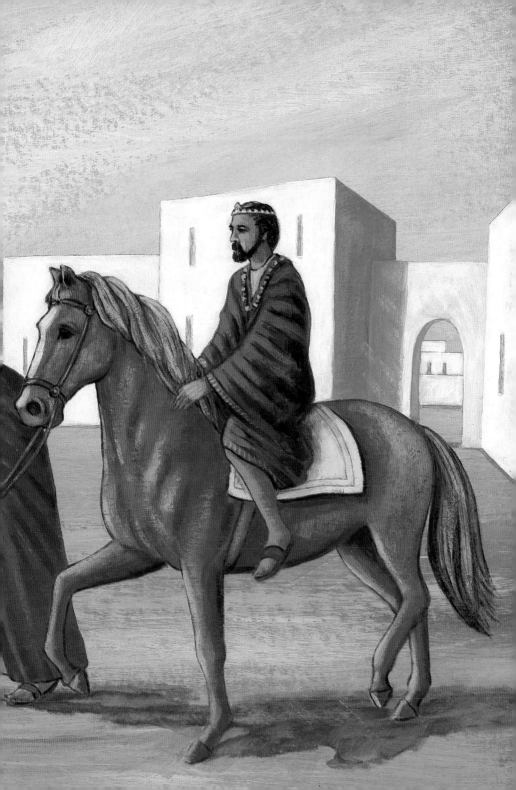

"This wicked man Haman," declared Esther.

Haman was terrified. The king was so angry, he went out into the palace garden. Haman turned to Esther and begged her to be lenient with him, but the king was enraged as he thought Haman was trying to hurt Esther.

"Haman has made gallows to hang Mordecai on," the king was told. "Hang Haman on them instead," he ordered.

King Ahasuerus gave Haman's property and lands to Esther. Esther told the king that Mordecai was her cousin. Mordecai was given Haman's ring and Esther made

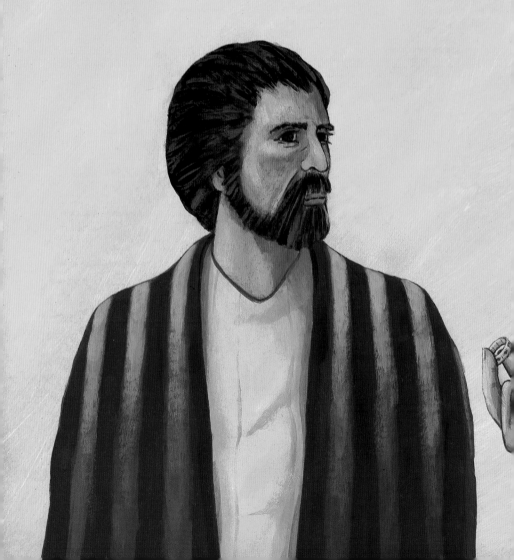

Mordecai the manager of Haman's estate.

Esther begged the king to reverse the orders that Haman had sent round the country.

So the royal scribes were called to write another letter to be sent to all the corners of the kingdom. The letter was sealed with the king's ring and sent out by messengers on fast horses, or mules, or young camels.

The Jews were to have power over the other people in the land instead of being subject to them.

Mordecai was highly honored by the king. He was given a blue and white robe and a crown of gold. He was next in importance to the king.

The Jewish people were very glad
and had many celebration feasts
and sent presents to one another.

What Esther did is still remembered
by Jews to this day.

But what God did for them is even
more important. He has the lives of
all men in His hands. What we
sometimes think is chance, is really
God's providence working.

The Bible tells us that "ALL THINGS
work together for good to them that
love God."

Previously published as:

REBEKAH: THE MOTHER OF TWINS, Copyright © 1985 by Christian Focus Publications Ltd.
HANNAH: THE MOTHER WHO PRAYED, Copyright © 1983 by Christian Focus Publications Ltd.
ESTHER: THE BRAVE QUEEN, Copyright © 1988 by Christian Focus Publications Ltd.

First Inspirational Press edition published in 1998.

Inspirational Press
A division of BBS Publishing Corporation
386 Park Avenue South
New York, NY 10016

Inspirational Press is a registered trademark of BBS Publishing Corporation.

Published by arrangement with Christian Focus Publications Ltd.,
Geanies House, Fearn, Tain, Ross-shire IV20 1TW, Scotland, UK.

Library of Congress Catalog Card Number: 97-77414
ISBN: 0-88486-203-8

Printed in Mexico.